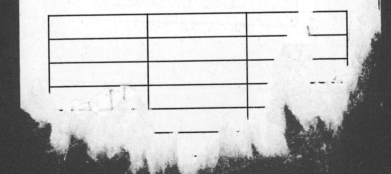

We Are All Born Free is illustrated by:

John Burningham, Niki Daly, Korky Paul, Jane Ray, Marie-Louise Fitzpatrick,
Jan Spivey Gilchrist, Ole Könnecke, Piet Grobler, Fernando Vilela, Polly Dunbar,
Bob Graham, Alan Lee, Hong Sung Dam, Frané Lessac, Sybille Hein,
Marie-Louise Gay, Jessica Souhami, Debi Gliori, Satoshi Kitamura, Gusti,
Catherine and Laurence Anholt, Jackie Morris, Brita Granström, Gilles Rapaport,
Nicholas Allan, Axel Scheffler, Chris Riddell, Marcia Williams

Cover illustration by Peter Sis

First published in Great Britain and in the USA in 2008 by
Frances Lincoln Children's Books, 4 Torriano Mews,
Torriano Avenue, London NW5 2RZ

www.franceslincoln.com

British Library Cataloguing in Publication Data
available on request

ISBN: 978-1-84507-650-4

Printed in Singapore

1 3 5 7 9 8 6 4 2

WE ARE ALL BORN FREE

The Universal Declaration of Human Rights in Pictures

F

FRANCES LINCOLN
CHILDREN'S BOOKS

In Association with Amnesty International

In January 2006 I published a novel called *The Boy In The Striped Pyjamas*. It was about two nine-year-old boys whose lives change for ever at the outbreak of the Second World War when they are caught up in one of the most horrible crimes that the world has ever seen.

Of course, the war took place before Amnesty International was set up and before the rights listed in this book were written down, so the characters in my story suffered in ways that no one ever should.

I've been lucky enough to talk to children all over the world about my book and whenever I do, I try to explain to them why the characters in my novel were treated so cruelly during those terrible years.

And I always come back to the Universal Declaration of Human Rights, the thirty rules that apply to everyone the world over and not just to those who share our place of birth, our colour or our religion.

Believing in them, acting on them, promising never to break them, that's how we make the world a better place. It's how we make ourselves better people. It's not all that complicated when you think about it, is it?

I hope you enjoy this book.

It might be the most important one that you ever own.

Photo by Kenneth Kyle Dundas

I've spent the last three years being part of a television programme called *Doctor Who*. I play a character called The Doctor who travels through time and space in a battered old wooden box. He's 903 years old and he comes from a planet called Gallifrey in the constellation of Kasterborous, but although he couldn't be less human I suspect he's got a copy of the Universal Declaration of Human Rights pinned up in his bedroom in the Tardis. Wherever he goes in the universe, he spends his time rooting out injustice and wrongdoing. He believes that everyone everywhere has the right to be happy and free – just as Amnesty International believes.

When I first heard about Amnesty International I was a teenager, just beginning to take an interest in what was going on in the world and continually shocked at how cruel and selfish human beings could be to each other. Amnesty International represented such a simple idea: that everyone everywhere deserved to be treated fairly.

The Universal Declaration of Human Rights is clear and uncomplicated. It reads like a list of common sense – maybe everyone should have a copy pinned up in their bedroom.

None of us are going to make it to 903 years old, so don't we all deserve to make the most of the time we've got? There are so many of us humans squeezing on to this wee planet and there's no Tardis coming to spirit us away. We need to look after each other.

In this beautiful book you'll find thirty rules for the world to live by.

We're all in it together.

Enjoy.

We are all born free and equal.

We all have our own thoughts and ideas.

We should all be treated in the same way.

These rights belong to everybody,
whatever our differences.

FREE TO DREAM

NELSON MANDELA OUR HERO

and to live in freedom and safety.

Nobody has any right to
MAKE US A SLAVE.

We cannot make
ANYONE ELSE OUR SLAVE.

Everyone has the right

to be protected by the law.

THE LAW IS THE SAME FOR EVERYONE.
IT MUST TREAT US ALL FAIRLY.

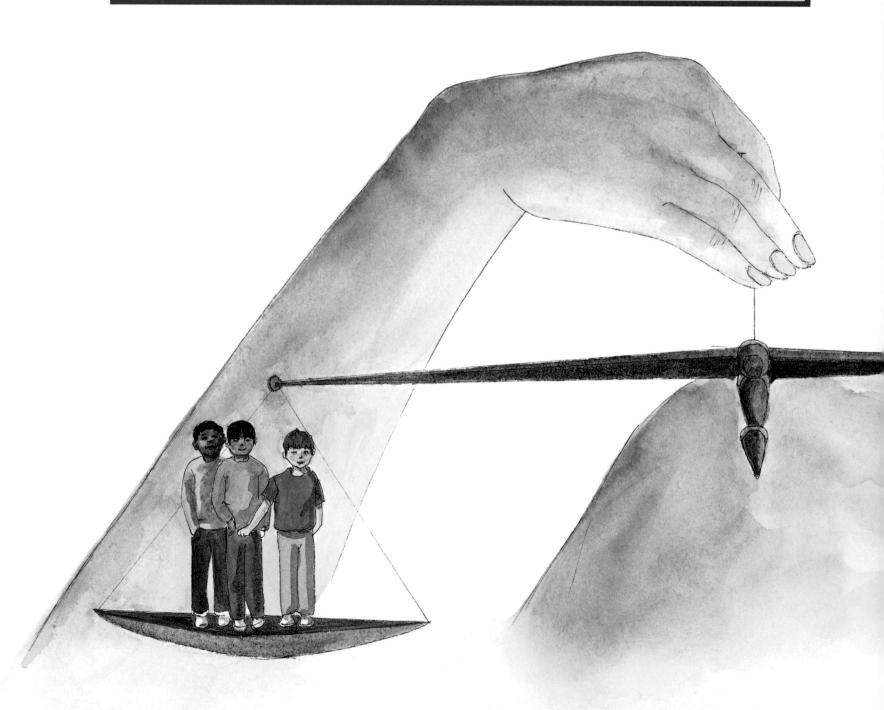

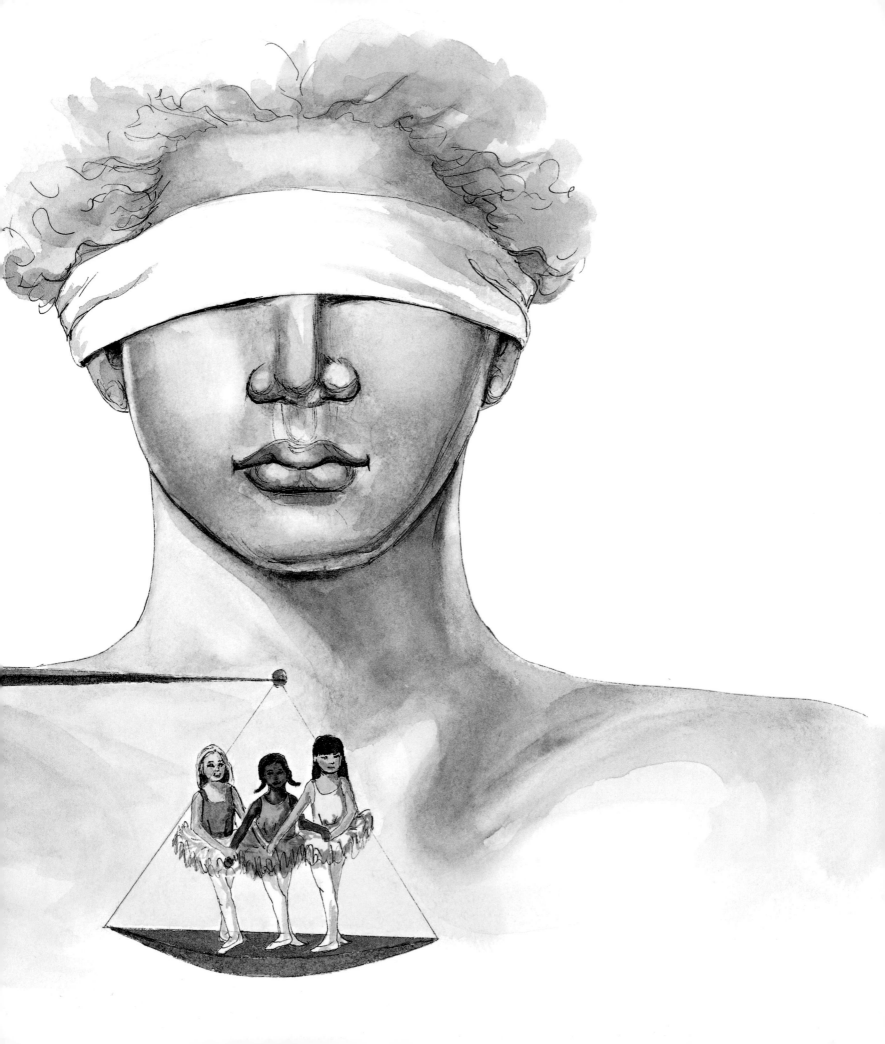

WE CAN ALL ASK FOR THE LAW TO HELP US

WHEN WE ARE NOT TREATED FAIRLY.

Nobody has the right to put us in prison
without a good reason, to keep us there
or to send us away from our country.

If we are put on trial, this should be in public.
The people who try us should not let anyone
tell them what to do.

Nobody should be blamed for doing
something until it is proved.
When people say we did a bad thing
we have the right to show it is not true.

Nobody should try to harm our **good** name.
Nobody has the right to come into our home,
open our letters, or bother us or our family
without a good reason.

We all have the right to go
    where we want in our own country
        and to travel abroad as we wish.

If we are frightened of being badly treated
in our own country, we all have the right
to run away to another country to be safe.

We all have the right to belong to a country.

Every grown up has the right to marry
and have a family if they want to.

Men and women have the same rights
when they are married, and when they are separated.

Everyone
has the right
to own things
or share them.
Nobody
should take
our things
from us
without a good reason.

We all have the right to believe in whatever we like, to have a religion, and to change it if we wish.

We all have the right to meet
our friends and to work together
in peace to defend our rights.
Nobody can make us join a group
if we don't want to.

We all have the right to take part in
the government of our country.
Every grown up should be allowed
to choose their own leaders.

Every grown up has the right to a job,
to a fair wage for their work,
and to join a trade union.

We all have the right
to rest from work
and relax.

We all have the right to a good life.
Mothers and children
and people who are old,
unemployed or disabled
have the right to be cared for.

We all have a right to education and to finish primary school which should be free.

We should be able to learn a career or make use of all our skills.

Our parents have the right to choose how and what we learn.

We should learn about the United Nations and about how to get on with other people and to respect their rights.

We all have the right
to our own way of life,
and to enjoy the good things
that science and learning bring.

Nobody can take these rights and freedoms from us.

THE UNIVERSAL DECLARATION

Article 1   We are all born free and equal. We all have our own thoughts and ideas.
We should all be treated in the same way.

Article 2   These rights belong to everybody, whatever our differences.

Article 3   We all have the right to life, and to live in freedom and safety.

Article 4   Nobody has any right to make us a slave. We cannot make anyone else our slave.

Article 5   Nobody has any right to hurt us or to torture us.

Article 6   Everyone has the right to be protected by the law.

Article 7   The law is the same for everyone. It must treat us all fairly.

Article 8   We can all ask for the law to help us when we are not treated fairly.

Article 9   Nobody has the right to put us in prison without a good reason,
to keep us there or to send us away from our country.

Article 10   If we are put on trial, this should be in public. The people who try us
should not let anyone tell them what to do.

Article 11   Nobody should be blamed for doing something until it is proved.
When people say we did a bad thing we have the right to show it is not true.

Article 12   Nobody should try to harm our good name. Nobody has the right to come
into our home, open our letters, or bother us or our family without a good reason.

Article 13   We all have the right to go where we want in our own country and to travel abroad
as we wish.

Article 14   If we are frightened of being badly treated in our own country,
we all have the right to run away to another country to be safe.

Article 15   We all have the right to belong to a country.

Article 16   Every grown up has the right to marry and have a family if they want to. Men and
women have the same rights when they are married, and when they are separated.

OF HUMAN RIGHTS

Article 17 Everyone has the right to own things or share them.
Nobody should take our things from us without a good reason.

Article 18 We all have the right to believe in whatever we like, to have a religion,
and to change it if we wish.

Article 19 We all have the right to make up our own minds, to think what we like,
to say what we think, and to share our ideas with other people.

Article 20 We all have the right to meet our friends and to work together in peace
to defend our rights. Nobody can make us join a group if we don't want to.

Article 21 We all have the right to take part in the government of our country.
Every grown up should be allowed to choose their own leaders.

Article 22 We all have the right to a home, enough money to live on and medical help
if we are ill. Music, art, craft, and sport are for everyone to enjoy.

Article 23 Every grown up has the right to a job, to a fair wage for their work, and to join a trade union.

Article 24 We all have the right to rest from work and relax.

Article 25 We all have the right to a good life. Mothers and children and people who are old,
unemployed or disabled have the right to be cared for.

Article 26 We all have a right to education and to finish primary school which should be free.
We should be able to learn a career or make use of all our skills. Our parents have
the right to choose how and what we learn. We should learn about the United Nations
and about how to get on with other people and to respect their rights.

Article 27 We all have the right to our own way of life, and to enjoy the good things
that science and learning bring.

Article 28 There must be proper order so we can all enjoy rights and freedoms
in our own country and all over the world.

Article 29 We have a duty to other people, and we should protect their rights and freedoms.

Article 30 Nobody can take these rights and freedoms from us.

Now meet the artists!

ARTICLES 1 & 2 – John Burningham has enjoyed international acclaim since his first book, *Borka: The Adventures of a Goose With No Feathers* won the Kate Greenaway Medal. He lives with his family in London.

ARTICLE 3 – Niki Daly is a renowned illustrator and writer who lives in Cape Town, South Africa. He has won many awards for his work that celebrates life and the on-going changes in his country.

ARTICLE 4 – Korky Paul was born in Zimbabwe and studied Fine Arts. Known only to himself as the 'World's Greatest Portrait Artist', Korky visits schools promoting his passion for drawing. He lives in Oxford.

ARTICLE 5 – Jane Ray is the illustrator of many distinguished and internationally-acclaimed picture books. She enjoys music, reading and gardening, and lives in North London with her husband, three children and two cats.

ARTICLE 6 – Marie-Louise Fitzpatrick is an award-winning Irish author/illustrator living in Dublin. Her books include *Silly Mummy, Silly Daddy, Izzy and Skunk* and *I'm a Tiger Too*.

ARTICLE 7 – Jan Spivey Gilchrist is an award-winning artist who has been inducted into the National Literary Hall of Fame for Writers of African Descent. She lives in the USA.

ARTICLE 8 – Ole Könnecke is a German author who grew up in Sweden. He began to draw while studying German Philology. He lives in Hamburg, Germany.

ARTICLE 9 – Piet Grobler grew up on a farm in the Limpopo province of South Africa. He now lives in Stellenbosch, and his work is published throughout the world.

ARTICLE 10 – Fernando Vilela is an award-winning Brazilian artist, designer, author and illustrator. He lives in São Paulo. His books include *The Great Snake: Stories from the Amazon*.

ARTICLE 11 – Polly Dunbar has written and illustrated many stories for children. Her book *Penguin* won the Silver Medal in the Nestlé Children's Book Prize. When she is not drawing, she likes to make puppets.

ARTICLE 12 – Bob Graham, Australia's leading picture-book artist, has written and illustrated many children's stories including *Rose Meets Mr Wintergarten, Buffy, "Let's Get a Pup!"* and its sequel, *"The Trouble with Dogs!"* He has won the Nestlé Children's Book Prize for *Max*, the Kate Greenaway Medal for *Jethro Byrde, Fairy Child*, and the Australian Children's Book of the Year Award four times.

ARTICLE 13 – Alan Lee has had a lifelong fascination with myths and fantasy. In addition to his award-winning books, he worked for 6 years on designs for the *Lord of the Rings* film trilogy.

ARTICLE 14 – Hong Sung Dam is an artist from South Korea. He was put in prison and tortured for his paintings and was an Amnesty International 'prisoner of conscience'. He was freed after four years.

ARTICLE 15 – Frané Lessac lives in Western Australia. In her books she aims to inspire children to learn about their own unique heritage using words and pictures.

ARTICLE 16 – Sybille Hein is the three-times winner of the Austrian Children's Book Prize. When she isn't drawing, she whizzes through the sandpits of Berlin with her little son, Mika.

ARTICLE 17 – Marie-Louise Gay has illustrated or written over sixty books for children. She also writes and designs puppet plays. She lives in Montréal, Canada.

ARTICLE 18 – Jessica Souhami's bold collage illustrations are influenced by her work as a shadow puppeteer. Her many children's books tell stories from around the world.

ARTICLE 19 – Debi Gliori was born and lives in Scotland. She began her career in 1984, and is now the author/illustrator of over sixty picture books, six novels, and she has five children.

ARTICLE 20 – Satoshi Kitamura was born in Tokyo, Japan. He is the illustrator of many award-winning books including the classic picture book *Angry Arthur*. He lives in London.

ARTICLE 21 – Gusti was born in Argentina and lives in Spain. An internationally-acclaimed artist, he is committed to the conservation of eagles in South America and condors in Argentina.

ARTICLE 22 – Catherine and Laurence Anholt have produced 100 bestselling children's books and have won numerous awards including the Nestlé Children's Book Prize on two occasions. They are the owners of *Chimp and Zee, Bookshop by the Sea* in Lyme Regis – the UK's first author-owned bookshop.

ARTICLE 23 – Gilles Rapaport lives in Paris, France. He is the illustrator of over 20 books for children. His work expresses his wish for children to realise the importance of being free in both mind and body.

ARTICLE 24 – Jackie Morris wanted to be an artist from the age of six. Now her books and paintings attract fans from all over the world. She lives in Pembrokeshire, Wales, in a small cottage by the sea.

ARTICLE 25 – Brita Granström grew up in Sweden but now lives and works mostly in Berwick-upon-Tweed, England with her husband, the writer and illustrator Mick Manning. She has won many awards for her picture books including the Nestlé Children's Book Prize Silver Medal and the Oppenheim Platinum Award.

ARTICLE 26 – Nicholas Allan wrote his first novel aged fourteen. His celebrated books – including *The Queen's Knickers* – have been translated into many languages, and his *Hilltop Hospital* is a BAFTA-award winning TV show.

ARTICLE 27 – Axel Scheffler was born in Hamburg, Germany, and now lives in the UK. He is an internationally-acclaimed artist who is best known for illustrating *The Gruffalo,* by Julia Donaldson.

ARTICLE 28 – Chris Riddell is a renowned illustrator and political cartoonist. His work is filled with fascinating detail and fantasy elements. His books include the Nestlé Book Prize Gold award-winning *Ottoline and the Yellow Cat*.

ARTICLES 29 & 30 – Marcia Williams has loved books from a very early age, and still remembers the joy of being read to. Her distinctive comic-strip illustration style is much admired all over the world. She lives in London.

The Universal Declaration of Human Rights looks after all of us, no matter who we are or where we live.

These rights were proclaimed by the United Nations on 10 December 1948, when the world said 'never again' to the horrors of the Second World War. Governments all over the world promised that they would tell people about these rights and try their best to uphold them.

Every child and grown-up in the world has these rights. We are all born free and equal. Our rights are part of what makes us human and no one should take them away from us.

Amnesty International works to protect our human rights, all over the world.

You can find out more at www.amnesty.org.uk/myrights

Amnesty International UK
17-15 New Inn Yard
London EC2A 3EA
tel: 020 7033 1500
www.amnesty.org.uk

Amnesty International USA
5 Penn Plaza, 16th Floor,
New York NY 10001
tel: (212) 807 8400
www.amnestyusa.org

Amnesty International Canada
(English-speaking)
312 Laurier Avenue East
Ottawa
Ontario K1N 1H9
tel: (613) 744 7667
www.amnesty.ca

Amnesty International Australia
Locked Bag 23,
Broadway,
New South Wales 2007
tel: 1300 300 920
www.amnesty.org.au